21st CENTURY INVENTIONS

INVENTIONS for BUSINESS, INDUSTRY, and the ENVIRONMENT

WORLD BOOK

www.worldbook.com

Co-published by agreement between Shi Tu Hui and World Book, Inc.

Shi Tu Hui
Room 1807, Block 1,
#3 West Dawang Road
Chaoyang District, Beijing 100025
P.R. China

World Book, Inc.
180 North LaSalle Street
Suite 900
Chicago, Illinois 60601
USA

© 2025. All rights reserved. This volume may not be reproduced in whole or in part in any form without prior written permission from the publisher.

WORLD BOOK and the GLOBE DEVICE are registered trademarks or trademarks of World Book, Inc.

Library of Congress Control Number: 2024943014

21st Century Inventions
ISBN: 978-0-7166-5360-8 (set, hard cover)

Inventions for Business, Industry, and the Environment
ISBN: 978-0-7166-5362-2 (hard cover)
ISBN: 978-0-7166-5368-4 (e-book)
ISBN: 978-0-7166-5365-3 (soft cover)

WORLD BOOK STAFF

Editorial

Vice President
Tom Evans

Senior Manager, New Content
Jeff De La Rosa

Manager, New Product Development
Nicholas Kilzer

Content Creator
Elizabeth Huyck

Writers
William D. Adams
Lauren Kelliher
Fred Maxon
Jenna Neely

Proofreader
Nathalie Strassheim

Indexer
Nathaniel Lindstrom

Graphics and Design

Senior Visual Communications Designer
Melanie Bender

Digital Asset Specialist
Rosalia Bledsoe

Acknowledgments
Designer: Starletta Polster
Writer: Alex Woolf

CONTENTS

3D printing	4
5G wireless	8
Automated waterway cleanup	10
Blockchain	12
CAPTCHA's	14
Carbon capture	16
Chip cards	18
City air purifier	20
Computer image recognition	22
Coworking spaces	26
Cryptocurrency	28
Drones	30
Electric cars	34
Electronic payments	38
Floating solar power	40
Forest city	42
Goal-line technology	44
Gorilla Glass	46
Gott-Goldberg-Vanderbei map projection	48
Graphene	50
Great Green Wall	52
High-speed maglev trains	54
High-speed rail	56
Lightweight laptops	58
Megatall skyscrapers	60
Paywalls	64
QR codes	66
RFID tags	68
Streaming services	70
Tidal energy	72
Video conferencing	74
Wind farms	76
Index	78
Acknowledgments	80

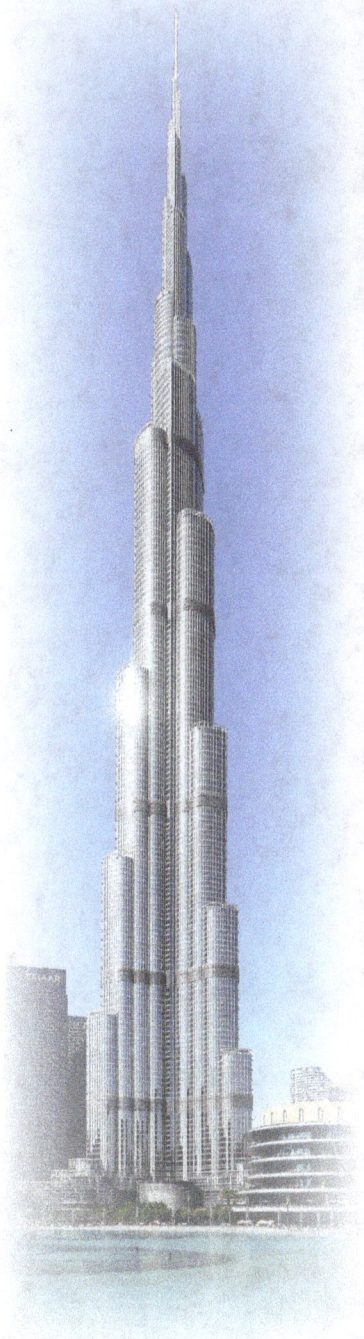

3D PRINTING:
The future manufactured to order

When the printing press was invented, it changed history. The ability to quickly print books instead of copying each one by hand meant knowledge and ideas could spread more easily. For hundreds of years, "printing" meant using ink to reproduce an image or words on paper. But 3D printers make objects, not words.

3D printing uses thin streams of hot plastic to build up objects layer by layer. First, users design the object using computer-aided design (CAD) software. In addition to designing objects, CAD software is used by engineers and architects to design buildings, bridges, and other projects. Once the object is designed, the CAD software produces a special file that will tell the 3D printer how to make the object.

Custom 3D bones

3D printing has found many new uses in medicine. One of these is printing scaffolds for growing bone. These printed bones are designed to provide a shape for natural bone to grow into. As new bone grows, the 3D-printed bone is reabsorbed by the body.

3D printers come in many sizes. Home 3D printers fit on a desk. Inside the printer is a flat printing surface and a moveable plastic-melting nozzle called the extruder. Extruders push strings of plastic through a narrow hole. A heat source near the hole melts the plastic just enough to bend and shape before it cools. The extruder runs on tracks that allow it to move up and down and side to side, controlled by a computer and motors.

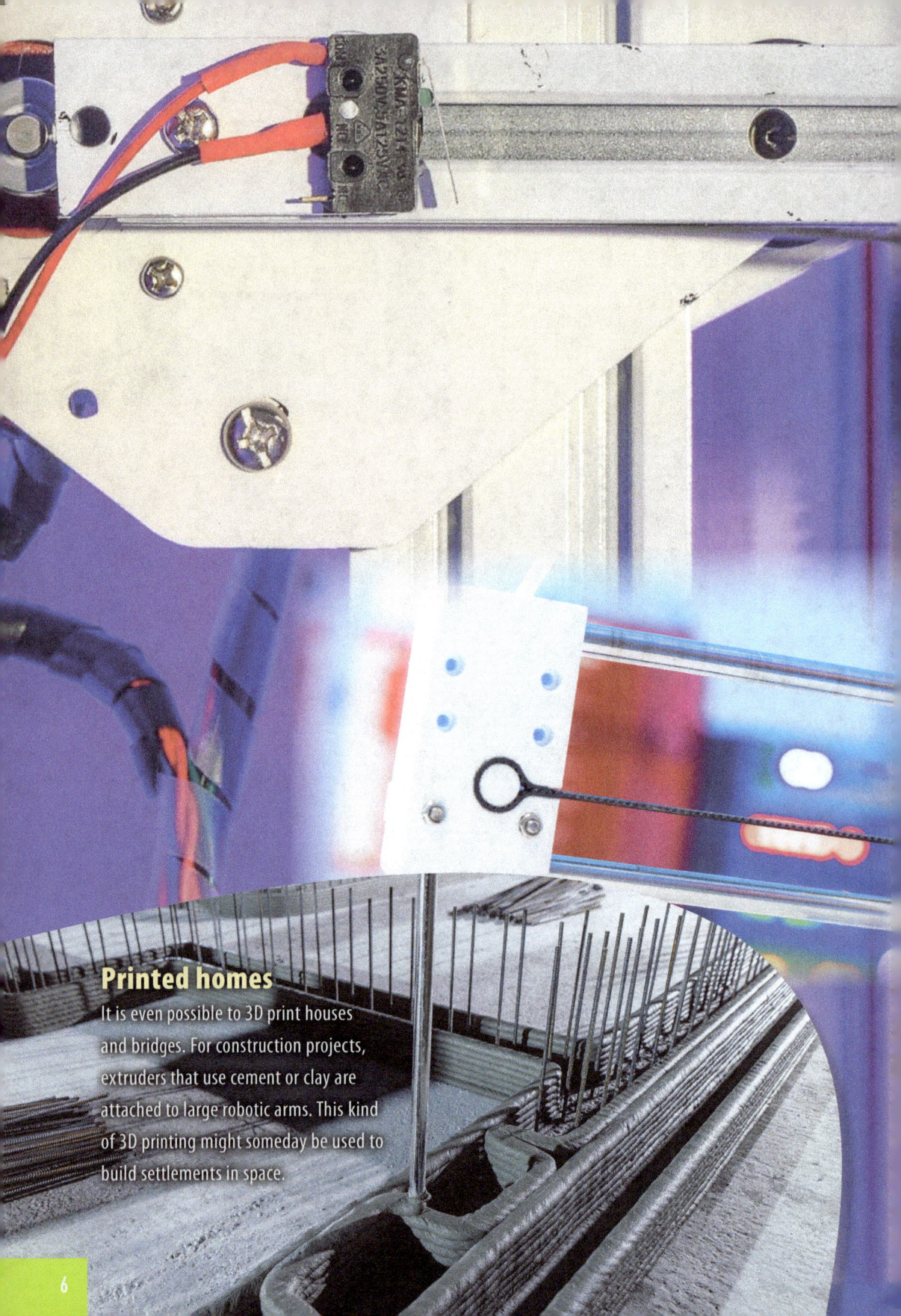

Printed homes

It is even possible to 3D print houses and bridges. For construction projects, extruders that use cement or clay are attached to large robotic arms. This kind of 3D printing might someday be used to build settlements in space.

Once the printer is warmed up, it's ready to print. It does this by spitting out plastic in very thin layers to build up the object, like constructing a loaf of bread by piling up slices. The computer file tells the printer where to spit plastic for each layer.

As it reads the file, the printer's motors move the extruder back and forth like a lawn mower, spitting out plastic at some spots. Then it moves up a bit to make the next slice.

The thinner the layers, the longer it will take to print, but the smoother the finished object will be. Depending on what you've designed, it may take a few hours to print. Larger objects need bigger printers, or they can be printed in pieces.

Designers can share or sell design plans on online forums. Often these plans can be edited, scaled, and customized. 3D printing has become a popular way to create items to sell online because they can be printed on demand.

3D printing isn't limited to just plastic objects. Scientists have used a similar process to print new organs for people in need of transplants. Organ bioprinting builds up organs using a substance called bioink. Bioink is made from a patient's living cells and a gel containing water and nutrients, such as collagen. The cells are collected from healthy tissue and grown in a pressurized container. Once there are enough cells to print the organ, technicians load a cartridge of bioink into a special 3D printer. It can take a few hours for the organ to be printed. On average, it takes about a month from collecting a cell sample to having the organ ready for transplant.

5G Wireless:
A better connection

Do you use a smartphone? You may be taking advantage of the fastest mobile data technology ever invented—5G. 5G networks are faster and more reliable than previous technology. That means clearer calls, fewer service interruptions, and fast streaming.

5G stands for the *fifth generation*. The technology is the fifth generation of *cellular service*, the technology that makes mobile phones work. A cellular network is divided into areas called *cells*. Within each cell, phones use radio waves to communicate with a base station. A base station handles all the communication within the surrounding cell. Base stations can hand communications off to one another, enabling mobile devices to move between cells.

No interceptions
The true test of a mobile network is how it handles large crowds. 5G technology has been successfully tested at National Football League games, with tens of thousands of fans (and their phones) packed into the stadium.

Each generation of cellular technology can handle faster communications and connect more devices. 5G can download data up to 100 times faster than the previous technology, 4G. 5G can also support up to 2.5 million devices per square mile (1 million per kilometer).

5G works in part by taking advantage of three different sets of radio waves, called frequency bands. Some bands are better at transmitting lots of data very quickly. Others are good at carrying messages over long distances. 5G uses a mix of high, mid, and low frequency bands to improve network coverage.

5G networks went live in 2019, and now more and more devices are built to use it. But 5G is not just about faster web surfing. It also improves the response time of banking and emergency systems.

5G networks are designed to limit small delays in device communications, called *latency*. High data speeds and low latency are necessary for some new technology, such as virtual and augmented reality. Low latency is also helpful for self-driving cars, where a lag might have life-or-death consequences.

Added security

5G uses stronger *encryption* than previous technology. Encryption means transmitting messages in code to protect information from data thieves. The added security is especially useful in online banking and telehealth.

AUTOMATED WATERWAY CLEANUP:
Gone fishing… for trash!

What is the best way to clean up a big mess? Get robots to do it!

About 33 billion pounds (15 billion kilograms) of plastic enter the ocean each year. Plastic pollution can harm animals and destroy habitats. It can also harm people when they swim in polluted waters or eat contaminated seafood. But how to get plastics out of the water? Automated waterway cleanup devices do just that: they filter and remove plastics from rivers, lakes, and the ocean.

The Seabin device was first used in Australia in 2016. It looks a bit like a trash can crossed with a pool skimmer. A Seabin floats in a polluted waterway, drawing in water with its solar-powered pump. A mesh catches the plastic and other trash. It can even catch *microplastics,* tiny particles of plastic that are particularly harmful. The filtered water is returned to the waterway. The latest model of Seabin can filter 1.4 million quarts (1.3 million liters) of water each day.

The waterway cleanup device known as Mr. Trash Wheel started gobbling up litter in 2014 in Baltimore, Maryland. It is a *semiautonomous* (partly robotic) 14-foot (4-meter) wheel. The wheel turns rakes and a conveyor belt that scoop up floating debris. The collected trash is then burned to generate electricity.

Mr. Trash Wheel was invented by the company Clearwater Mills. To draw the public into the cleanup, they gave the wheel googly eyes, a name, and plenty of personality.

Mr. Trash Wheel removes hundreds of tons of trash from the water every year. On one banner day, it collected 38,000 pounds (17,000 kilograms) of trash. Mr. Trash Wheel now has company. An entire family of Trash Wheels works to keep trash out of the city's harbor.

Microplastics, major problems

Tiny plastic bits, called microplastics, can kill fish and leach poisons into the water. The Ocean Health Lab, which opened in 2022 in Sydney, Australia, is devoted to studying the problem of ocean plastic.

Dumpster diving

The Trash Wheel family has raked in hundreds of thousands of plastic bags, almost 2 million plastic bottles, more than 1 million foam containers, and thousands of sports balls. But Mr. Trash Wheel's googly eyes have seen some weirder things scooped up, including live snakes and a guitar.

BLOCKCHAIN:
Keeping data secure

Imagine a number trick that could keep your data private, protect banks, and prevent fraud in elections. It exists, and it's called blockchain.

Blockchain is not a device. It is an algorithm, a way of storing information in a computer. Normally, when we share digital information, anyone can change it later. Blockchain is different. It is shared in a way that makes it impossible to alter. This way, the information remains secure.

Blockchains are often used for buying or selling. A blockchain is simply a ledger of every transaction, as if each person who used a dollar bill added their initials. Details of each transaction are recorded in *blocks*, chunks of code linked up in a chain. The ledger is distributed, meaning it is shared among many different computers on a network.

Each block contains a timestamp and the hash of the previous block. A hash is a single number produced by running the block's code through a special math problem. Since each block includes the hash of the previous blocks, blocks cannot be added, removed, or changed without the change being noticed.

Blockchain is secure because it is distributed, and no single person (or node) on the network can alter information held within a block without everyone else being aware of it. Blockchain also doesn't depend on a single government or bank. Instead, the network of nodes must collectively approve the transactions that are added to the blockchain.

Origins

Researchers Stuart Haber and W. Scott Stornetta invented blockchains back in 1991. However, it wasn't until 2009, with the launch of Bitcoin, that blockchain found a real-world application.

Many potential uses

As well as cryptocurrency transactions, blockchain can be used to record many other kinds of information.

- Votes in an election could be recorded in a blockchain. Once cast, votes could not be changed, helping to eliminate fraud.

- Blockchain could enable food producers to track a product's progress at each stage from farm to shop, ensuring that nothing contaminates their products.

- If a patient's medical records are recorded and encrypted on a blockchain, it will help keep them private.

CAPTCHA'S:
Foiling the bots

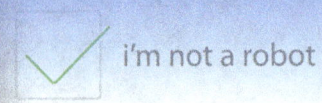

Type the two words:

Has a website ever asked you to pick out photos of traffic lights or type squiggly letters? Congratulations, you've just proved you're a human.

This type of test is called a CAPTCHA. They are designed to distinguish real human computer users from bots (automated software programs). The idea behind them is that there are some tasks, such as reading distorted letters, that are hard for bots but easy for a human brain.

Bots are automated programs that scan websites, sign up for fake accounts, and sometimes buy up all the concert tickets to popular concerts. Bots are also used to send spam mail to millions of people.

With advances in artificial intelligence (AI), bots are becoming better at passing CAPTCHA tests. Researchers have responded with new tests, called reCAPTCHA. These tests show a set of images and ask users to click the ones that contain a certain object, such as cars or traffic lights. If their response matches those of most other users, they pass the test.

Another reCAPTCHA test involves just checking a box marked "I'm not a robot." Of course, a bot could do that. But the program is sneaky. It actually looks at the movement of the cursor near the box. A human-controlled cursor will move in tiny, random ways that a bot cannot easily mimic.

The most recent forms of reCAPTCHA run in the background. They observe general behavior while visiting a website, including keystrokes and cursor movements. The reCAPTCHA allocates the visitor a score from 0.0 through 1.0. The lower the score, the more likely the visitor is a bot.

Turing test

CAPTCHA stands for Completely Automated Public Turing test to tell Computers and Humans Apart. The name refers to the British computer pioneer Alan Turing, who back in 1950 proposed a test to assess the abilities of artificial intelligence programs.

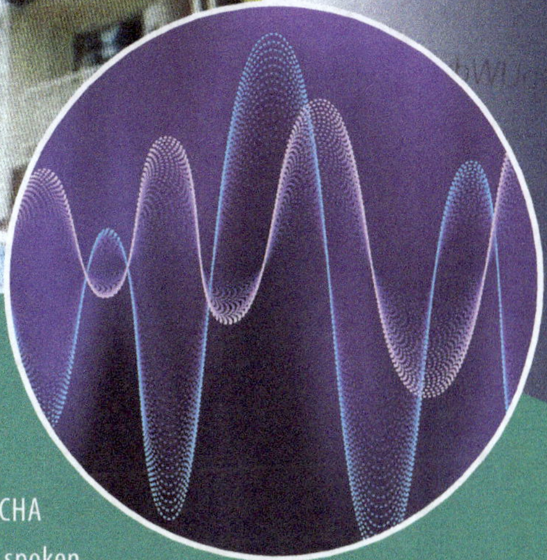

Audio versions

For the visually impaired, an audio CAPTCHA might ask the user to identify a series of spoken letters or numbers. Such tests often use a distorted voice or include background noise to foil voice-recognition programs.

CARBON CAPTURE:
Harnessing hope

Climatologists (scientists who study climate) agree: we're pumping too much carbon dioxide (CO_2) into the atmosphere. This is causing a rapid rise in average worldwide temperatures. Even if we stopped emitting CO_2 today, there's already enough in the atmosphere to change Earth's climate.

Solving this problem will take a multipronged approach including renewable energy, electric grid improvements, and battery technology. And to remove existing CO_2, engineers are turning to carbon capture technology.

The easiest place to stop CO_2 is before it gets into the air—in the chimneys of fossil fuel-burning power plants. In flue traps, CO_2-rich exhaust is bubbled through a solution called an *amine*. The amine traps the CO_2 and allows other gases to escape. Then the amine is heated to release the CO_2 into a holding tank.

Heating amine to release the CO_2 takes energy, cutting into the output of the power plant. Researchers are experimenting with different CO_2-absorbing solutions that might work better. For example, some have lower boiling points, so they require less energy to release the CO_2.

Other engineers are designing facilities to pull CO_2 directly from the air, called direct air capture (DAC). The CO_2 can be stored, converted to other chemicals, or even used in products!

DAC would need to happen at an enormous scale to have any impact on the climate. But every bit helps. The first large-scale DAC plant, called Orca, opened in Iceland in 2021. It captures 4,000 tons of CO_2 per year. It's a start!

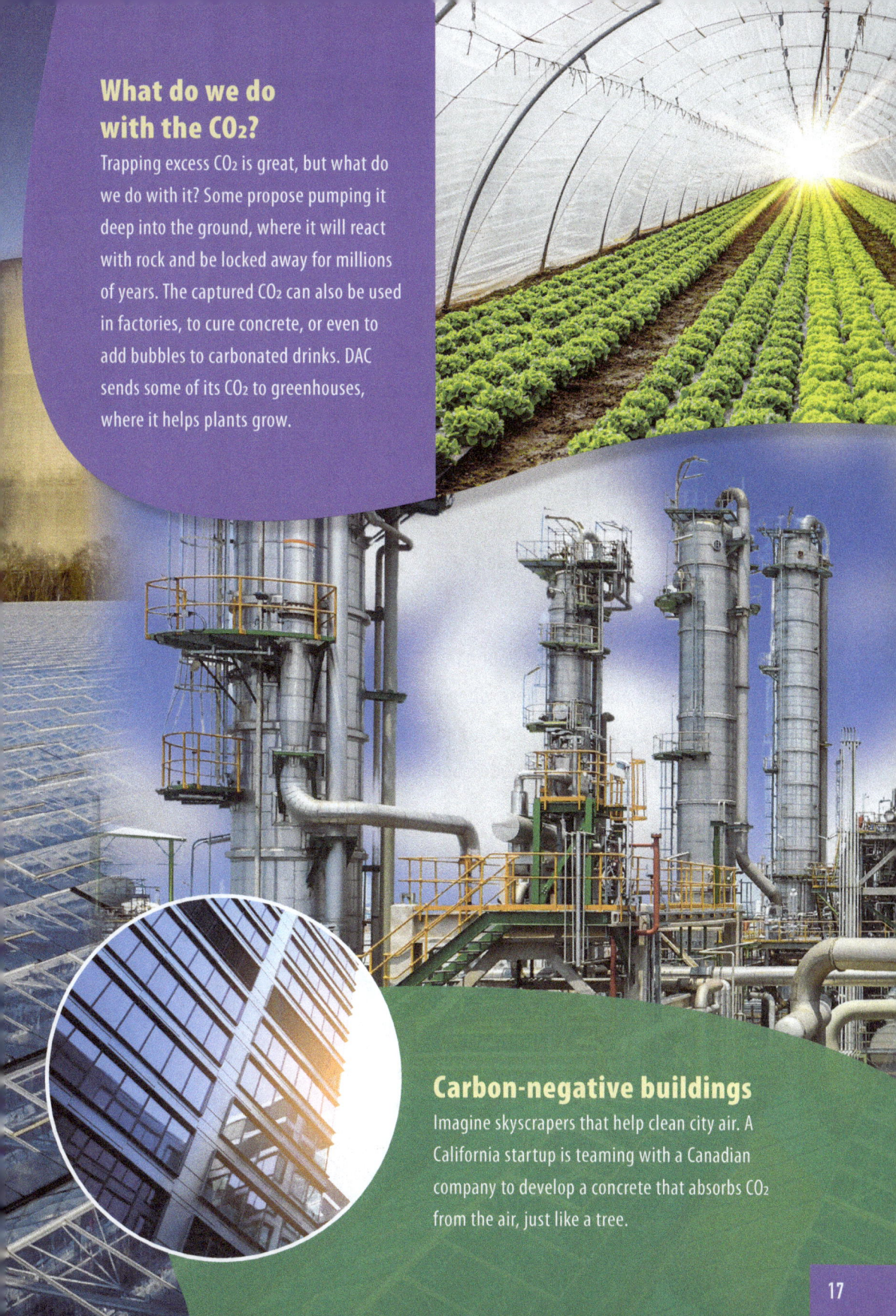

What do we do with the CO₂?

Trapping excess CO$_2$ is great, but what do we do with it? Some propose pumping it deep into the ground, where it will react with rock and be locked away for millions of years. The captured CO$_2$ can also be used in factories, to cure concrete, or even to add bubbles to carbonated drinks. DAC sends some of its CO$_2$ to greenhouses, where it helps plants grow.

Carbon-negative buildings

Imagine skyscrapers that help clean city air. A California startup is teaming with a Canadian company to develop a concrete that absorbs CO$_2$ from the air, just like a tree.

CHIP CARDS:
Smarter and safer

When you tap a credit card on a screen or slide it into a slot to pay for something, the transaction is handled by a small metal square embedded in the card. That's the chip in a chip card.

Chip cards make it much harder to steal your personal information. Chips are found in credit cards, debit cards, and ATM cards. Chip cards are sometimes called smart cards—with good reason!

Bank cards store information, such as your name and credit card number, and share these when you tap or swipe the card. Before chips, cards stored this data in a magnetic stripe on the card's back. Some cards still have these stripes as a backup.

Chip cards store your information in a microchip embedded in the plastic. A chip can hold more information than a magnetic stripe can. The chip is not powered by a battery in the card. Rather, the power comes from the device used to read the card.

Chips vs. stripes

A common magnetic-stripe identification card might hold a person's name, address, government identification number, and insurance information. That information can easily be taken by thieves. Thieves can also *clone* a magnetic-stripe card by copying the information onto their own card. Chip cards can also be cloned, but it is much harder.

Chip cards encode all your personal information in a one-time transaction code before sharing it with a vendor. These codes change every time the card is used, so if a store's data gets stolen, hackers will not get your personal information or be able to use your card number. That keeps your money and identity safe.

Digital wallets on a smartphone or watch work like chip cards. They use the same technology to protect their data.

Gone global

EMV chip cards were first introduced in Europe in 1994. EMV stands for the financial companies Europay, Mastercard, and Visa. The security of chips quickly cut down on fraud. In 2015, banks in the United States started swapping their swipe cards for chip cards.

CITY AIR PURIFIER:
For a fresher metropolis

There is nothing like a breath of fresh air in the middle of a bustling city! But can cities clean their own breezes?

Air pollution is one of the biggest threats to human health. In 2018, the World Health Organization reported that 9 out of 10 people in the world breathe polluted air, and that air pollution is a factor in 7 million deaths per year.

Some engineers are attempting to solve the problem by building air purifiers for entire cities. These devices operate on solar power and suck out harmful contaminants from the air, returning fresh air to the surrounding area. They look like skyscrapers or large statues.

In 2016, engineers installed a giant air purifier in Xi'an, China. Standing 328 feet (100 meters) tall, the "smog tower" sits on top of a greenhouse. As the sun warms city air that has been sucked into the greenhouse, it rises through multiple HEPA filters in the tower before flowing back outside. HEPA stands for High-Efficiency Particulate Air. HEPA filters have layers of materials that trap harmful pollutants, allowing just air to flow through.

The Xi'an air purifier was specifically designed to catch air pollutants called PM2.5. These are tiny particles 2.5 microns or less in size, which can get deep into lungs and are especially harmful. PM2.5 makes up most smog, making the air appear hazy and reducing visibility.

Blame the coal

Much of the air pollution in Xi'an comes from coal burned to power factories and generate electricity. Coal is a dirty fuel that creates smog when it is burned. Xi'an residents often wear protective face masks in the cold months when coal-burning heating systems create choking smog. If coal is used as fuel, the smog will continue.

Another kind of smog tower has been installed in Tianjin, China, and Krakow, Poland. These towers use electrostatic filters. Electrostatic filters ionize, or charge, the particles in the air and then attract them to metal plates, allowing cleaned air to pass through. Engineers are working on systems that can span larger areas across a city.

Delhi's biggest fan

The city of Delhi, India, installed a smog tower in a busy market area in 2021. It uses 40 giant fans to suck in polluted air through 5,000 filters to clean it. However, the tower runs on electricity generated by burning coal, which produces more smog.

Computer image recognition:
Machines that see

Standing in your backyard, you spot something dark up in a leafy tree. It's a bird—a red-breasted sapsucker. Humans, like many animals, are very good at spotting and identifying objects. We take this skill for granted, but teaching it to a computer is extremely difficult. Even distinguishing an object from its background is a major challenge to a machine.

Computer image recognition is a technology that enables machines to recognize objects in images and classify them (put them into their correct class or group). Computers do this using artificial intelligence (AI). By being shown thousands of images containing labeled objects, they start to "learn" what everything from birds to pizzas to mountains looks like.

The form of AI used in computer image recognition is called a convolutional neural network (CNN). A CNN is made up of many layers. The higher layers work on identifying the basic elements of the image, including edges, borders, and simple shapes. Deeper layers search for more subtle patterns, such as the eyes of a dog, the feathers of a bird, or the leaves of a tree. The CNN assigns a score to each object based on its confidence that it has correctly identified it.

Often, it makes mistakes. Some classes of objects—dogs, for example—can vary widely in shape, size, and color. They look different from different angles or in poor light, or they might be behind another object. But the more images the CNN is shown, the better it will get at identifying them.

Space exploration

Curiosity, NASA's uncrewed rover, is exploring the surface of Mars. Computer image recognition enables it to identify scientifically valuable targets to investigate.

Pixels

The human eye sees each object as a single thing. Computers, however, break images into tiny square dots called pixels. They give each pixel a numerical value based on how dark or light it is. They use this to make predictions about the picture. It is the location, pattern, and intensity of pixels that a computer analyzes when it attempts to identify objects.

Recurrent neural networks (RNN's) are like CNN's but can process a series of images to find the connections between them. These are used to analyze videos. RNN's can, for example, track an object such as a vehicle as it moves through traffic.

Optical character recognition (OCR) recognizes the images of letters. It converts printed or handwritten text into electronic text. It can also be used to read road signs and vehicle license plates.

Computer image recognition has many useful applications. It can be used to search the internet for images of particular people or objects. Self-driving cars use it to identify traffic signals, road markings, bicycles, and pedestrians. Manufacturers use computer vision to check for blemishes or breakages in their products, which saves having to hire someone to stand at a production line and look at each item.

And maybe someday your phone will be able to look at a photo of your room and point to where you left your keys.

Facial recognition

Computer vision that is trained to recognize faces can be used as a security tool. Everyone's face is unique, making it a kind of built-in password. Security cameras with facial recognition software can identify people allowed to enter an area, or look for a wanted person in a crowd. Some can even estimate emotional states by analyzing facial expressions and body language, which can reveal if someone is angry, nervous, or scared.

The birth of computer vision

In 1957, a team of American computer scientists led by Russell A. Kirsch built the first image scanner, a machine that could convert a picture into a grid of pixels with numerical values that a computer could understand. The first ever digital image was a photo of Kirsch's infant son. Soon, researchers were creating algorithms that could detect simple things like edges, corners, and curves. However, this took huge amounts of processing power. In the 2010's, advances in AI combined with faster processing speeds allowed computer image recognition to take off.

Coworking spaces:
Productive communities

Do you wish you had an office, a quiet place to get some work done? Now, you can rent one.

Coworking spaces rent work spaces to people without access to a traditional office. These might be remote workers, *entrepreneurs* (business starters), or *freelancers* (people who don't work for a single company but take on projects for different businesses). The people in a coworking space do not all work for the same employer. Instead, individuals and groups can rent desks, meeting rooms, and other facilities.

Many coworking spaces create a welcoming environment by providing wireless internet, private rooms, and snacks and coffee. Some also try to encourage interaction between people in different lines of work.

Your interior design
Each coworking space has its own style. Some are funky and industrial. They may appeal to entrepreneurs and creative freelancers. Others are more polished and clean. You can choose the style that suits you!

The first coworking space opened in 2002 in Vienna, Austria. The goal was to bring entrepreneurs and other creative people together to *collaborate* (work together). The idea spread to San Francisco, California, in 2005. Coworking spaces offered a place that wasn't the garage for new businesses without much cash to get started.

The COVID-19 pandemic disrupted traditional office work in 2020. Offices were shut down for long periods. Some workers found that they could be just as productive working from home over the internet. But coworking spaces are another option.

Why leave home to go to a coworking space? Homes can be full of distractions and interruptions from roommates and family members. For parents, they provide a work space separate from demanding children. Other people like the social and creative opportunities that coworking spaces provide.

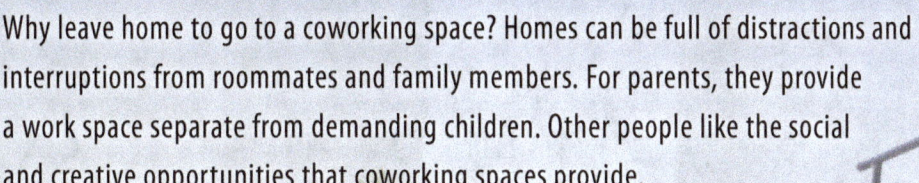

Makerspace

Another type of collaborative work environment is called a *makerspace*. Here, the focus is on making things. Makerspaces often provide 3D printers, laser cutters, and other advanced tools to help people create their wildest dreams!

CRYPTOCURRENCY:
The future of money?

When you buy something in a store, you pay for it with a currency, such as the U.S. dollar, which is backed by the government. That is why storekeepers trust it. For centuries, that is how money has worked—until the arrival of cryptocurrencies.

Cryptocurrencies are something new. They are backed by no government, bank, or central authority. Instead, the value of a cryptocurrency is controlled by the users themselves. They are called cryptocurrencies because they use *encryption* (converting data into a secret code) to make transactions secure.

Unlike traditional money, cryptocurrencies do not have physical notes or coins. Cryptocurrency "coins" exist only in digital form. The coins are created using a process called mining. This involves using computers to solve difficult mathematical problems. People can also purchase cryptocurrency coins from other cryptocurrency holders.

Cryptocurrency coins are stored in a digital "wallet." The wallet is an app on a computer that holds the keys that give users access to their coins. Wallets contain a public key (the wallet's address) and private keys, known only to the owner, which they need if they want to buy something with their cryptocurrency. Cryptocurrency transactions are recorded in a special kind of digital file called a blockchain (see pages 12-13).

One problem with all forms of money is inflation, which happens when there is too much money in circulation, and it loses its value. The creators of cryptocurrencies have attempted to avoid the problem of inflation by limiting the number of coins that can be mined and put into circulation. For example, in the case of the cryptocurrency Bitcoin, no more than 21 million coins will ever be mined.

What can you buy with cryptocurrency?

Cryptocurrencies are not widely used for day-to-day shopping because most stores will not accept them. However, you can spend them at some technology companies, gaming sites, and luxury stores. Many people buy cryptocurrency not to spend but as an investment, in the hope that it will go up in value.

Bitcoin

The first cryptocurrency was Bitcoin, created in 2009 by a person or group calling themselves Satoshi Nakamoto. Since then, many other cryptocurrencies have been developed, such as Ethereum, Litecoin, and Ripple, but Bitcoin remains the most popular and valuable. Bitcoins are getting steadily harder to mine. It is estimated that the last one will be mined in 2140.

DRONES:
Unmanned and on a mission

Is that a bird? Or a plane? Or maybe a drone?

A drone, also known as an unmanned aerial vehicle (UAV), is a flying robot without a pilot. Most are small, although they can be as large as a full-sized plane. Drones are used in the military, surveillance, filming, and even for deliveries!

The earliest UAV's were balloons and kites equipped with cameras. In the 1900's, radio-controlled unmanned aircraft were used to take photos of enemy locations, act as decoys in battle, and to drop bombs and missiles.

Modern military drones became common in the 2000's. A Chinese company started making small drones for civilian use in 2012. But the United States did not allow commercial drones until 2017.

Drone bodies are made from light metals, carbon fiber, and plastics. The materials must be light, to allow the aircraft to fly, but strong enough to withstand weather and crashes.

Drones come in many different designs, depending on how they will be used. They might have a single rotor or many, a fixed wing or a mix of rotors and wings. Quadcopters, with four rotors, are a popular model. Drones with rotors can take off and land vertically. If one of the rotors fails, the drone can still navigate an emergency landing. The pilot steers the drone by controlling the engines moving the rotors.

Drones run on electric batteries. As batteries improve, drones will be able to fly longer distances without charging.

Drones are usually operated by a pilot on the ground with a remote control or smartphone app. The operator can direct a drone where to go, or give it instructions to fly *autonomously* (without human control). The control device tracks the drone's altitude, speed, and battery charge. It also shows the view from any onboard camera and collects data from sensors carried on the drone.

A buzzword

The word "drone" was first used to describe an unmanned aerial vehicle in 1946. Drones are male bees, which do not sting or make honey but follow the queen bee, like a UAV follows its pilot's instructions. The name also fits the high-pitched noise they make.

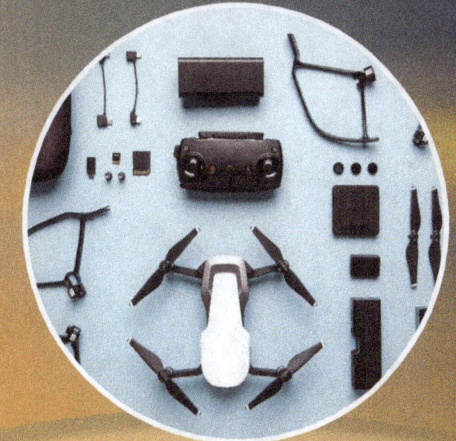

Tracking poachers

Conservationists use drones with *infrared* (heat-sensing) cameras to track poachers. Poachers often move at night to illegally hunt wild animals. Poaching occurs worldwide and threatens the survival of many endangered species, such as elephants and rhinoceroses.

Most drones carry lightweight digital video cameras. The camera on the drone sends a live video feed to the remote control, allowing the pilot to see what the drone sees and steer the drone from below.

Drones are very useful in many professions. They can go where humans can't, and are often a safer, less expensive, and more efficient way to scan large areas. Farmers use drones to inspect and monitor crops. After disasters, emergency response teams use drones to look for people in distress and survey damaged homes. Scientists use drones to monitor potential landslides, volcanic eruptions, erosion, caves, and flooding. Drones can also collect soil and water samples, monitor animal populations, and make detailed maps.

Drones can help inspect buildings and bridges, especially parts that are hard or impossible for human inspectors to reach. They have been used for aerial photography for real estate, marketing, sporting events, and mapping and surveying. Some companies use drones to deliver medical supplies and small packages. Schools use drones to explore the environment and learn about robotics and the physics of flight.

And as drone technology improves, we may soon see more of them in the sky!

Tiny but mighty

The Massachusetts Institute of Technology (MIT) is developing insect-sized drones to help with rescue efforts following earthquakes. This micro-drone is about the size of a dragonfly and weighs as much as a paper clip. It can maneuver into tight spaces to search for earthquake survivors in collapsed buildings.

Tesla's drone boat

Famed inventor Nikola Tesla created a remote-controlled boat in 1898. He controlled the model boat using radio signals. The U.S. military started experimenting with remote control about 20 years after Tesla's demonstration.

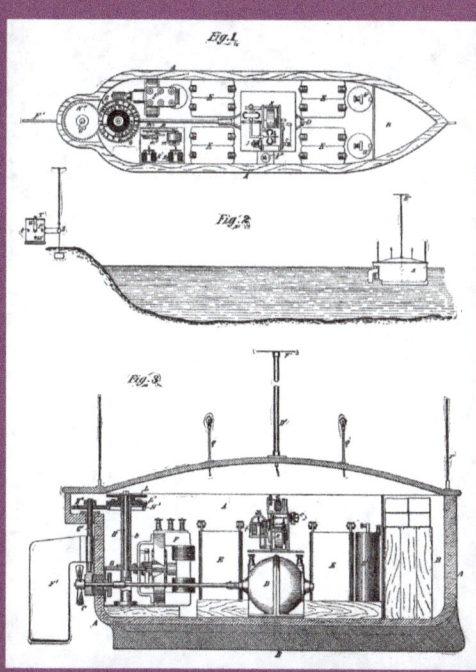

Electric cars:
Better batteries

One hundred years ago, electric cars were all the rage. They were quiet, easy to drive, and best of all, did not spit out smelly exhaust. Fast-forward to today, and electric vehicles (EV's) are back and better than ever. Now EV's account for about 5 percent of worldwide passenger vehicle sales, but that number is rising fast.

Electric cars look like any other car on the market. But instead of burning gasoline, they are powered by rechargeable batteries. Most EV's today use lithium-ion batteries that fill the base of the car. EV's charge by plugging into a socket. Fuel cells—devices that store chemical energy in the form of compressed hydrogen—can also power electric vehicles.

Electric cars are designed so that little energy is wasted. When the vehicle brakes, the wheel motors turn into generators, sending electric power back to recharge the batteries. This process, called regenerative braking, reduces the energy needed to drive the car. EV tires are inflated to a higher pressure than tires on gas cars. This means the car can roll with less effort, saving energy. The tires are also self-sealing, so there is no need to carry a spare. Even the car windows help. They are made of solar glass that keeps the car from getting too hot or cold, without running the heater or air conditioning.

Electric origins

Scottish inventor Robert Anderson created the first electric carriage between 1832 and 1839. Around the same time, American blacksmith Thomas Davenport created a battery-powered electric motor. He attached it to a car on a train track. His invention led to the development of electric streetcars and the electric locomotive.

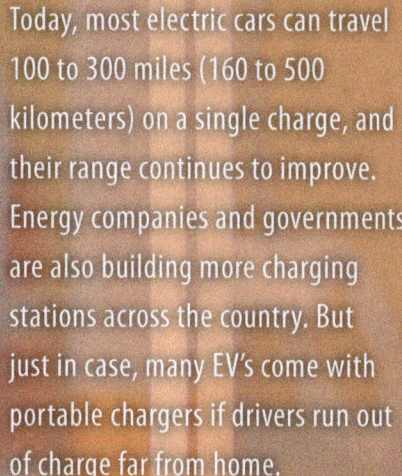

Today, most electric cars can travel 100 to 300 miles (160 to 500 kilometers) on a single charge, and their range continues to improve. Energy companies and governments are also building more charging stations across the country. But just in case, many EV's come with portable chargers if drivers run out of charge far from home.

Lunar sparks

In 1971, during the Apollo 15 mission, the first crewed vehicle to drive on the moon was an electric car called the Lunar Roving Vehicle. This space-age rover gave electric cars a popularity boost back on Earth.

It takes only a few minutes to fill the gas tank on a typical car. Charging an EV takes longer—sometimes a lot longer. Charging time is a concern that keeps some buyers from trying an EV. But new fast-charging stations have cut charging times considerably. They can provide a full charge in 20 to 30 minutes, just enough time for a snack.

EV's produce no exhaust, meaning they don't emit carbon dioxide or polluting particles. Of course, the electricity to charge the batteries may still come from power plants that burn coal and other fossil fuels, reducing the environmental benefits. But EV's are almost always more energy-efficient than gas cars, as well as cleaner. They convert a higher percentage of energy from the grid into motion than gasoline vehicles.

The lithium-ion batteries used in most EV's are expensive. They also require mining and processing the metals lithium, cobalt, and nickel, which can harm the environment. Engineers are looking for ways to reuse or recycle old EV batteries to make them more environmentally friendly. But there are still some challenges to solve before EV's completely replace gasoline vehicles.

Trip planning

If you're planning a long trip in your EV, an EV trip planner app can give you a route showing when and where to recharge the battery. The route factors in how much energy the battery will use, when it might run down, and which charging stations your model can use.

Sound off on

Electric vehicles are quiet—sometimes too quiet. As of 2020, the European Union and the United States require all new electric cars to produce a sound that warns of their approach. The added noise helps cyclists, pedestrians, and people who are blind notice the car and stay safe.

Electronic payments:
Money on the go!

With a few clicks on a website, you can buy a new toy, a book, or something to wear. Apps on smartphones make it simple to order taxis or take-out. All these things cost money. But how does the money get paid?

You could give the online store your credit card number. But if you'd rather keep that private, you can pay through an electronic payment service, such as PayPal.

PayPal was founded in 1998 and became popular thanks to such online auction websites as eBay. Before PayPal, buyers had to send sellers a check or money order, then trust that they would mail the item. PayPal offered a safer way. It served as a middleman, using Electronic Funds Transfers (EFT's) to transfer money safely without revealing personal banking information. In 2002, PayPal became eBay's official payment provider.

With the rise of smartphones around 2010, such financial apps as Venmo and Cash App let people transfer small amounts to friends. This made it easy to split a bill or pay a small business. Venmo transactions can be immediately transferred to your bank for a small fee or can be sent for free if you wait a few days.

Venmo had more than 90 million users in the U.S. by 2022. Many stores are now adding QR codes to items to make it easier to check out

Busy banking

In the 25 years since it was founded, there have been over 25 billion payment transactions through PayPal. In this time, users have made over $1.5 trillion in payments.

using the Venmo app. Other apps, such as Cash App, also let you buy and sell stocks, and both Venmo and Cash App let you use cryptocurrency in transactions.

Apple developed its own mobile payment service, Apple Pay, in 2014. It allows users to make payments using their Apple devices.

Zelle is a popular mobile payment service that arrived in 2017. It allows users to send and receive money directly from their bank accounts. Developed by a group of U.S. banks, Zelle offers a secure way to transfer funds between friends, family, and businesses using a smartphone.

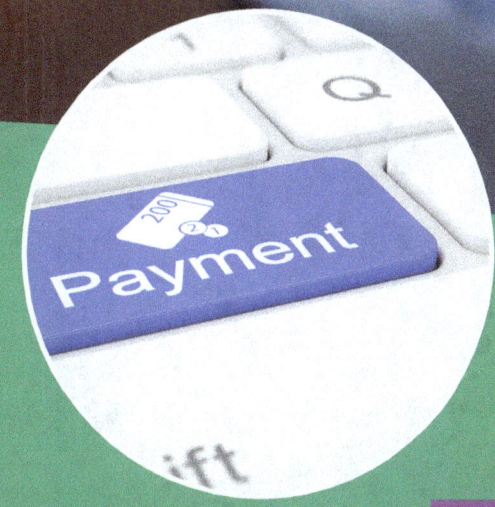

Hey, big sender!

For verified users, it is possible to send up to $60,000 every week on Venmo before you hit their limit. If a person is not verified, they are capped at $299.99.

Floating solar power:
Where sun meets the sea

The world is slowly flowing to renewable energy sources, and more countries are considering floating solar power. Solar power produces renewable, clean energy. But solar panels can take up a lot of space. So why not put them on the water?

Earth gets a huge amount of energy from the sun. Solar energy cells collect the sun's energy and change it into electric power.

Large solar cells can provide electric power for homes and other buildings.

Most solar panels are installed on land. But placing solar cells over water has several advantages. First, when solar panels overheat, they do not perform as well. The cooling effect of water helps solar panels produce more usable energy.

Floating barriers

Floating solar energy systems have many benefits, but there are also challenges. The solar panels must be anchored and tilt at just the right angle to catch the sun's rays. In the ocean, saltwater may corrode wiring and electronics. Freshwater solar systems may compete with fishermen, recreational boaters, and swimmers for space.

Floating solar panels also free up land for other uses, such as growing crops or carbon-absorbing forests. Solar power cells can even float on hydropower reservoirs, industrial ponds, or near-coastal areas.

Hydroelectric dams are the world's largest renewable energy source, but they may be less effective during drought. But floating solar panels on a hydropower reservoir can generate solar power to supplement the energy supply. Covering only 3 to 4 percent of the reservoir with solar panels can potentially double the amount of electricity produced by the plant.

Covering farm reservoirs with solar panels can provide energy to pump water and irrigate fields. The solar panels also help reduce water loss through evaporation.

Follow the sun

A Dutch floating solar power system called Proteus follows the sun throughout the day to get maximum rays. The single-sided panels slowly rotate every few hours. They have sensors that track the sunlight and tilt the panels to catch the sun at the best angle.

The panels even improve water quality by discouraging the growth of toxic algae that can harm humans and animals.

In 2006, solar power accounted for 0.03 percent of the world's electricity production. By 2022, that had grown to 3.6 percent. This will increase even faster as more solar power systems take to the water.

FOREST CITY:
Climate-friendly living

In the Guangxi region of southeastern China, an unusual group of terraced buildings covered in lush greenery blends in with the mountains. Construction started on the first forest city in the world, near Liuzhou, in 2020.

A forest city is an urban space with many plants and trees. The Liuzhou forest city runs along the Liujiang River for 432 acres (175 hectares). Plants of all sizes fill parks, gardens, and buildings. Inside the stepped towers are shops, apartments, hotels, hospitals, and a school. The nearby city of Liuzhou is connected to the forest city by a fast train and roads suited to electric vehicles.

The forest city is designed to absorb 10,000 tons of carbon dioxide from the air each year and generate 900 tons of oxygen. It will do this mostly with the power of green plants. Lush trees and bushes fill roofs and balconies and drip from buildings. All that greenery attracts small animals, birds, and bugs to make the forest city their home. The plants also absorb pollution, lower the temperature, and block city noise.

The forest city is also designed to be energy self-sufficient. Rooftop solar panels and geothermal energy power the buildings. Geothermal energy comes from Earth's heat. In the future, more cities may find that going green is a great way to build for a better life.

Italian origins

Italian architect Stefano Boeri originated the idea of a forest city in 2016 and designed two residential forest towers in Milan in 2021. The towers are home to 21,000 plants and 300 people. They are powered by renewable energy, and the plants are watered with filtered wastewater. His vertical forest design will be repeated in more cities soon.

Treehouse upgrade

Green city structures come in many shapes and sizes, but they all have large terraces for growing plants. In 2022, China built this home where shrubs and trees outnumber people 10 to 1.

GOAL-LINE TECHNOLOGY:
Did it cross the line?

You shoot. You score! Or do you? At the last moment, the goalkeeper tips the ball onto the crossbar. It bounces down and is kicked away. But did it cross the line? Everyone awaits the referee's decision.

For a goal to count, the whole of the ball must cross the line. This can be a tricky call for referees. They might be too far away or their view might be blocked by other players. When mistakes are made, players and fans get angry.

Today, many soccer leagues are turning to goal-line technology (GLT) to help referees make the right call. There are several types of GLT. Some use cameras, while others use electronic trackers inside the ball and the goal. One form of GLT is called Hawk Eye. This uses fourteen cameras placed in different positions around the stadium.

Hawk Eye software calculates the position of the ball relative to the goal line using a geometric technique called *triangulation*. By forming triangles between three points (two of its cameras and the ball), it uses the angles between them to determine the ball's precise location.

Hawk Eye can do the math and let the referee know where the ball landed within half a second. It only needs two cameras with good views to triangulate the ball's position, so it works even if some cameras are blocked by players.

High-speed cameras

A kicked soccer ball moves through the air at an average of 75 miles (120 kilometers) per hour. Standard video cameras operating at 25 frames per second are too slow to precisely track a ball at this speed. Hawk Eye uses cameras that operate at 500 frames per second, making it possible to track even the fastest kick.

Smart soccer ball

Another GLT system, called Cairos, uses thin cables buried around the penalty area and beneath the goal line. The electric current in the cables creates a magnetic field. A sensor inside the ball feels the magnetic field as the ball passes through it and transmits the ball's location. A computer can then determine whether the ball has crossed the line.

Gorilla Glass:
Tough as glass

Glass is fragile. It breaks into sharp tiny pieces when it hits the ground. So why do we cover cellphones with it? The answer is that the glass on smartphones, tablets, and other gadgets isn't just glass. It's super-tough: Gorilla Glass!

Gorilla Glass is chemically altered glass made by the Corning Corporation. Corning developed Gorilla Glass at the request of Apple founder Steve Jobs. He wanted a strong, thin glass for Apple's touchscreen products. Corning came up with Gorilla Glass. The tough new glass was used to make the touchscreens on the first iPhones in 2007.

Glass is made by melting together silica sand, soda ash (sodium carbonate), and lime (calcium oxide) in a hot furnace. The Gorilla Glass recipe also includes a bit of aluminum and magnesium. The *molten* (melted) glass is poured into a v-shaped trough until it overflows the sides. A robotic arm draws flat sheets of glass off the trough.

To turn regular glass into Gorilla Glass, the glass sheets are placed in a bath of molten potassium salt. This changes the chemical structure of the glass. Small sodium ions in the glass are replaced by larger potassium ions from the bath. The larger ions make the glass strong and crack-resistant by taking up more space. Finally, the glass is cooled and cut, ready to cover a phone.

Gorilla Glass is extremely thin, but it can survive falls from up to 2 meters onto hard surfaces. Gorilla Glass is almost as hard as a sapphire. That's why you can keep your phone in a pocket with keys and it doesn't get scratched!

Gorilla Glass protects more than six billion devices around the world. It is on smartphones, smart watches, tablets, and computers. Corning has improved its formulas over the years to become even more scratch-resistant, drop-proof, and thin.

Victus victory

Corning released its newest Gorilla Glass, called Victus 2, in 2022. If you want to drop your smartphone onto concrete without it breaking, Victus 2 is the glass for you!

Germ-free glass

Some Gorilla Glass has a thin coating of silver ions, which discourage bacteria from sticking to the glass. This keeps your phone from becoming a germ magnet!

Gott-Goldberg-Vanderbei MAP PROJECTION:

The globe in 2D

A globe is the most accurate way to view our round planet. But what's the best way to represent it on a flat map? This problem has vexed mapmakers for centuries.

The Gott-Goldberg-Vanderbei Map Projection is a new solution to this old problem. It is the most accurate 2D map of Earth ever made.

All maps that flatten out a round surface will stretch some areas and shrink others—an effect called distortion. Since 1569, many mapmakers have used a flattening method invented by the Flemish geographer Gerardus Mercator, called the Mercator projection. There are many others.

The Gott-Goldberg-Vanderbei projection was released in 2021. Its goal is to minimize distortion. The double-sided circular map looks like a globe squished flat. Astrophysicist J. Richard Gott and his colleagues David Goldberg and Robert Vanderbei created the map to accurately show the relative sizes and positions of Earth's continents. Their projection also better represents Earth's southern hemisphere.

To develop their projection, Goldberg and Gott created a system to score the accuracy of maps on six types of distortions: 1) area, 2) bending, 3) boundary cuts, 4) distances, 5) local shapes, and 6) lopsidedness. The lower

Stacks of maps

Two-sided Gott-Goldberg-Vanderbei maps can be overlaid to show different features. Several are currently offered free online. Different maps show national borders, climate zones, language groups, and historical events. Other maps show the moon, planets of our solar system, and the Milky Way galaxy.

the score, the more accurate the map. The score for a globe is 0.0. The Gott-Goldberg-Vanderbei projection has small distortions in all the categories, so they do not sacrifice accuracy in one category for another. Its error score is 0.881.

The projection was inspired by the designs of the American inventor Buckminster Fuller. In 1949, Fuller designed a map that could be folded into a *polyhedral* (many-sided) globe.

Purple people

Vanderbei created an election map for the United States. He dubbed it "Purple America." His map showed red, blue, and shades of purple (plus a little green). The colors represent how much one area voted for a political party by county. Vanderbei released maps for every U.S. presidential election from 1960 to 2020. It shows Americans are less divided by region than we think.

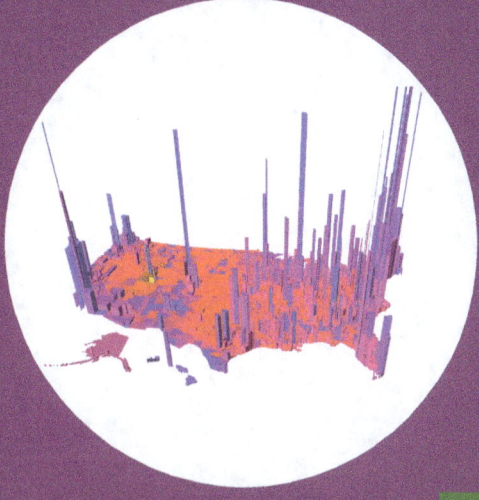

GRAPHENE:
The wonder material

Imagine a material lighter than a feather, yet stronger than steel. Sounds impossible? It's real, and it's called graphene.

Graphene is made entirely of carbon. Its single layer of carbon atoms is arranged in a tightly bound hexagonal lattice, like a honeycomb, giving it remarkable strength. Yet at just one atom thick, graphene is the thinnest material known to humans.

Electrons can flow among the carbon atoms, so graphene conducts electricity with little resistance and no heat. Thanks to this amazing property, graphene could be used to make batteries that charge faster and last ten times longer than lithium batteries.

Graphene has many other potential uses. It is transparent, making it ideal for touchscreens on mobile devices. It's also flexible, which could be useful for foldable phones. Combined with other materials, graphene could provide better thermal insulation for buildings, and make them more resistant to corrosion, dampness, and fire. Graphene could improve hearing aids and surgical implants. And it could make electronic circuits faster and waterproof.

The first graphene-based product to be manufactured was an antitheft device with graphene electronic circuitry, launched in 2011. Since then, graphene has appeared in enhanced tennis rackets, helmets, and ski equipment, as well as smartphones and noise-reducing foam covers for cars.

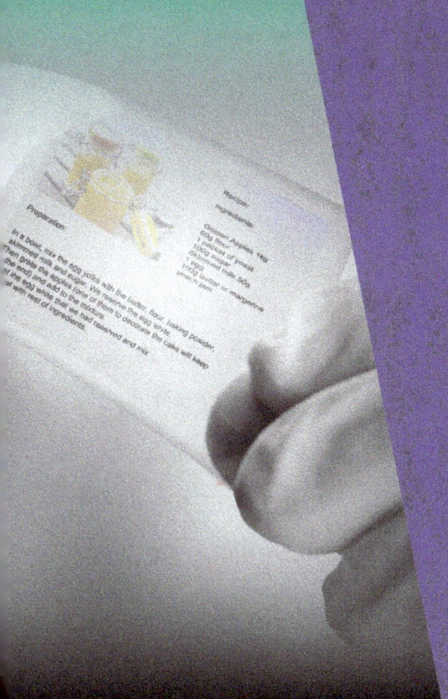

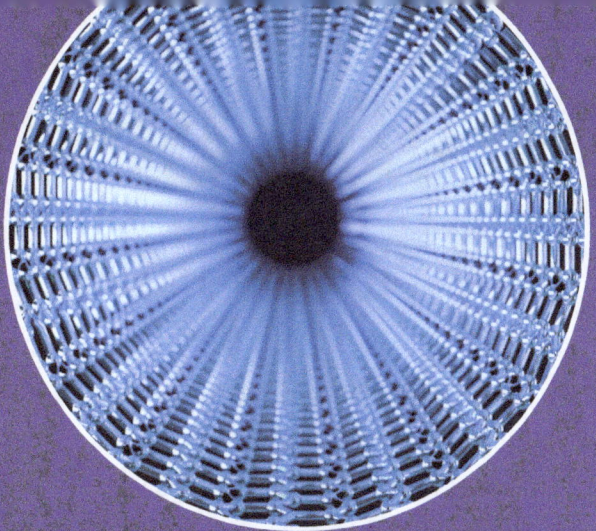

Remarkable discovery

In 2004, two scientists in the UK, Andre Geim and Konstantin Novoselov, were experimenting with graphite, the material used in pencils. They wanted to see if they could separate it into layers. Using ordinary sticky tape, they peeled off the top layer. Flakes of graphite came off. They stuck tape to those flakes and peeled again, and repeated the process ten or twenty times. The flakes coming off got thinner and thinner until eventually they were left with graphene, just one atom thick. By dissolving the tape in a chemical solution, the graphene could be isolated. In 2010, Geim and Novoselov were awarded the Nobel Prize in physics for their discovery of graphene.

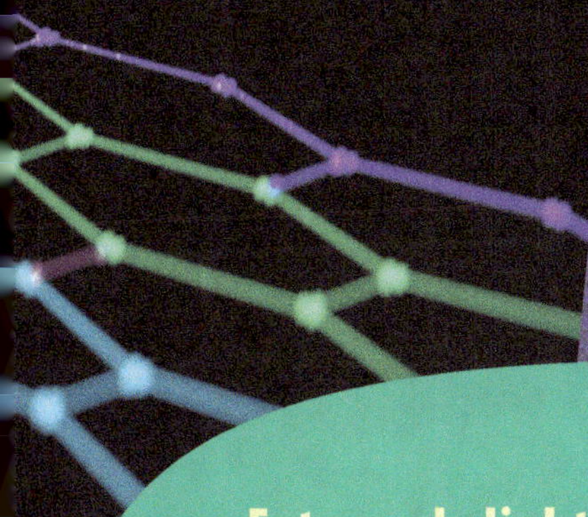

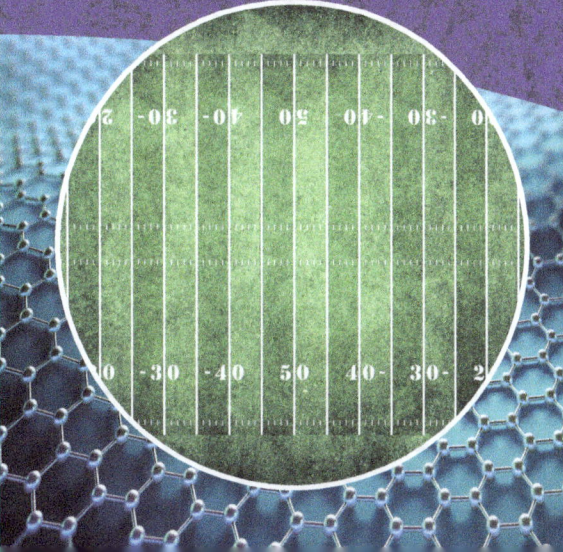

Extremely light

Graphene is the lightest material we know of. A single sheet of graphene big enough to cover a football field would weigh less than 0.035 ounce (1 gram).

Great Green Wall:
A growing world wonder

What is big, green, and changing the world? The Great Green Wall is a project to plant billions of trees and other plants in the Sahel region of Africa.

The Sahel is sandwiched between the grassy savanna region and the Sahara, the world's largest desert. The Sahara is expanding due to climate change and other factors. But countries in the region have teamed up to fight back.

The wall of trees is intended to fight *desertification*. Desertification is the loss of productive, fertile land to dry, desertlike conditions. Many factors contribute to desertification. They include climate change, extreme weather, deforestation, over-farming, and over-grazing. The Sahel is home to 500 million people. The effects of desertification threaten their survival.

A new wonder
The group building Africa's Great Green Wall hopes it will one day join the Great Wall of China, the Taj Mahal, and the Great Pyramid of Giza as a world wonder.

In 2007, 11 African countries joined together to combat desertification by planting trees and restoring native plants. They are Djibouti, Eritrea, Ethiopia, Sudan, Chad, Niger, Nigeria, Mali, Burkina Faso, Mauritania, and Senegal. Together, they form a horizontal line across the entire continent.

How can trees stop desertification? Trees act as windbreaks to keep the wind from blowing away topsoil. Their roots help store water in the ground. Roots also prevent soil from being washed away by heavy rains. Trees also absorb carbon dioxide from the air and provide shelter for wildlife.

The Great Green Wall is made up mostly of drought-resistant trees, such as acacia. Some of the trees are fruit-bearing, providing food.

The project hopes to create a belt of plant life at least 9 miles (15 kilometers) wide across the region by 2030. Countries are already seeing benefits. Millions of acres or hectares have been restored in Ethiopia and Nigeria, bringing green to land that was once in danger of becoming a desert.

A growing idea

China is building its own Great Green Wall. The country's Three-North Shelter Forest Program aims to plant 2,800 miles (4,500 kilometers) of trees by 2050 to hold back the Gobi Desert.

HIGH-SPEED MAGLEV TRAINS:
A magnetic adventure

Trains can get you to many places. But a high-speed maglev train can get you there faster.

Maglev stands for magnetic levitation. Maglev trains don't have engines. Instead, powerful magnets float them above the track and pull them along. That means they run quietly and smoothly at high speeds, up to 374 miles (601 kilometers) per hour.

The first commercial maglev train opened in 1984 in the United Kingdom. It ran at a low speed from the Birmingham train station to the airport for 11 years. The first high-speed maglev train was built in 2003 in Shanghai, China. The Shanghai maglev train is the fastest commercial train in the world. It carries passengers 18.6 miles (30 kilometers) from the airport to the metro station in seven minutes and 20 seconds.

If maglev trains don't have an engine, how do they go so fast? If you have played with magnets, you know that magnets either attract or repel each other. An electrical current will also create a magnetic field. Engineers used these simple concepts to design maglev trains.

Large superconducting magnets are attached to the underside of the train. A magnetized coil runs along the track. This coil and the magnets under the train repel each other, pushing the train up. The repulsion leaves a small gap of air between the train and the track, levitating the train. Electrified coils on the side of the tracks produce a magnetic field that travels along the track and pushes the train forward, much as an ocean wave pushes a surfer.

Maglev trains use powerful superconducting magnets. Superconductivity is the ability to conduct an electric current with very little resistance. This lack of resistance means they lose little energy and can produce powerful magnetic fields.

Pacemaker danger

A pacemaker is a medical device used to regulate a person's heartbeat. The strong magnetic fields surrounding maglev trains might interfere with pacemakers. Passengers with pacemakers should do their research before boarding a high-speed maglev train.

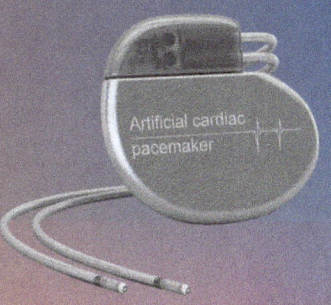

But these magnets must be cooled to -450 °F (-278 °C) to become superconductive.

The lack of friction and aerodynamic designs allow maglev trains to travel at high speeds. Imagine taking a train from Paris to Rome in two hours! However, maglev trains are costly to build, leaving the idea a dream for some countries. As of 2022, only six high-speed maglev trains run throughout the world. There are three in China, two in South Korea, and one in Japan.

Upkeep dream

Traditional trains need a lot of upkeep. Parts wear down and get damaged by friction and shaking. Although maglev trains are expensive to build, they are inexpensive to operate! Because the trains don't touch the tracks, parts do not wear down.

HIGH-SPEED RAIL:
Faster, smoother travel

Long trips can be dull. But soon they may get shorter—if you take the train. Fast train travel, known as high-speed rail (HSR), is becoming more common all over the world.

HSR is any train that runs at 124 miles (200 kilometers) per hour or faster. Some can reach twice that speed. HSR does not require magnets or other new technology—it is possible through improvements to existing trains and rails.

HSR tracks are *continuously welded,* meaning that the sections are seamlessly welded together. The base of the passenger compartment is fitted with air springs to absorb the vibrations of the wheels on the track. These innovations ensure that passengers have a smooth ride, even at very high speeds.

Today, most HSR trains are electrically powered from overhead lines. To help them achieve higher speeds, the front cars are often tapered like the nose of an airplane to minimize air resistance. HSR trains are designed to tilt when rounding curves to reduce rocking motions. Sensors feed information to a computer that controls the angle of tilt.

HSR trains travel too fast for drivers to read track signals, so information about track conditions, other trains, and braking is sent wirelessly to the driver's cab. If the driver does not respond to a message to slow down the train, a computer can do this automatically.

HSR in China

Since the start of the 21st century, China has become the world leader in the development of HSR. By 2023, China had two-thirds of the world's total HSR.

Japan's bullet train

The world's first HSR line was opened in Japan in 1964. This was the 320-mile (515-km) Shinkansen line, connecting Tokyo and Osaka. The trains were nicknamed "bullet trains" because of their long, tapered noses. Their top speed was 135 miles (220 kilometers) per hour.

Fastest trains

The current world speed record for an HSR train is 357.2 miles (574.8 kilometers) per hour, set by a French train on a special test track in 2007. The HSR speed record on a conventional track is 302 miles (486.1 kilometers) per hour, achieved in 2010 on the Beijing–Shanghai line.

Lightweight laptops:
Big power in a light package

Since the 1980's, personal computers have evolved from bulky desktop machines to sleek and lightweight devices, just right for laps.

All laptops are portable, but lightweight laptops are especially slim and light. A traditional laptop may weigh 4 to 7 pounds (1.8 to 3.2 kilograms). Lightweight laptops weigh half as much. First introduced around 2008, they are often preferred by people who want something bigger than a smartphone but lighter and thinner than a standard laptop.

Advances in computer technology, miniaturization, and new materials make lightweight laptops possible. The newest microchips pack more processing power into a fraction of the size. Lightweight laptops also reduce weight and size by replacing internal hard drives with flash memory, and removing such components as bulky CD drives and USB ports.

Lightweight laptops come in different forms. A folio-style laptop has a clamshell design, with a hinge below the screen that connects it to a keyboard. Other styles include tablet computers that come with detachable keyboards and stands. Convertible laptops can switch between tablet and folio style. Some lightweight laptops come with touchscreens.

Ultra lightweight laptops were more expensive when they were first introduced, but now they cost about the same as full-sized laptops—which have also gotten lighter.

Portable, in a sense

The first portable computer, the Osborne 1, was released in 1981. It weighed a whopping 24.5 pounds (11 kilograms) and had a 5-inch (12.7-centimeter) display, smaller than a Nintendo Switch. The Osborne 1 looked like a suitcase and came with a leather handle.

Apple slice

Apple first introduced its ultralight laptop in 2008. The MacBook Air weighed three pounds (1.4 kilograms) and was only 0.76 inch (1.93 centimeters) thick. Apple pared this laptop down to just the essential components, so it lacked an optical drive and Ethernet port.

Megatall SKYSCRAPERS:
Vertical cities towering above

Look up—and up—and up. Does that building ever end?

Megatall skyscrapers are the tallest buildings in the world, taller than 1,968.5 feet (600 meters). That is about 150 stories (floors)!

The first modern building to reach into the sky was the Home Life Insurance building, constructed in Chicago in 1885. It was a then-astonishing 10 stories (floors) tall. It used a new steel skeleton design, meaning the walls did not have to hold the building's weight. Since then, skyscrapers have stretched 20 times taller.

The current tallest building in the world is the Burj Khalifa, in Dubai, United Arab Emirates. It stands 2,716 feet (828 meters) tall. The Burj Khalifa was completed in 2010 and cost $1.5 billion. It has 163 floors and 57 elevators. The Burj Khalifa is made of aluminum, stainless steel, and glass. Its design uses bundled towers of different heights.

Unlike many skyscrapers, the Burj Khalifa does not have a steel frame. A core of reinforced concrete supports the building. The base of the building is shaped like a three-petaled flower. As the building rises, it thins. This design supports the weight and allows it to withstand high winds.

Megatall skyscrapers require some extraordinary engineering. Architects use a series of pillars and cores inside to stabilize them, called a tube system. Tall buildings also need to taper, with a base larger than the top, to support the sideways push of the weight.

Believe it or not, skyscrapers are designed to sway in the wind—but

Burj Khalifa

Growing pains

The Jeddah Tower in Jeddah, Saudi Arabia, is experiencing growing pains. It is the first skyscraper expected to reach 3,300 feet (1,000 meters). Construction began in 2013, but it has stalled since 2018. It currently stands at a quarter of its designed height.

Shanghai Tower

not too much. Large *dampers* high up in the building help keep them steady. Dampers are weights that move. When the building sways, the damper sways the other way, balancing the movement.

Megatall skyscrapers can add offices, stores, hotels, and apartments in crowded cities, while leaving space for more parks and other public spaces. Tall skyscrapers are also status symbols. They attract tourists and win records. Why aren't there more? Megatall skyscrapers cost billions of dollars and can take decades to build.

Ancient skyscrapers

For most of history, the tallest building in the world was the Great Pyramid of Giza, standing 481 feet (146.5 meters) tall. It was the tallest known structure until the construction of Lincoln Cathedral in the United Kingdom in 1311.

The Makkah Royal Clock Tower

The tallest building in Asia and the second tallest in the world is the Merdeka 118 in Kuala Lumpur, Malaysia. Completed in 2023, the Merdeka 118 rises 2,227 feet (678.9 meters) tall, with 118 stories. Different patterns and textures characterize the exterior, to reference Malaysian arts and crafts.

The world's third tallest building is the 2,073-foot (632-meter) Shanghai Tower in Shanghai, China. You may not notice how tall it is at first, because it stands next to two other supertall buildings! The Shanghai Tower is made of concrete and steel, surrounded by a glass skin that helps regulate temperatures inside. The glass is held in a steel frame that twists 120 degrees from the base to the top of the building. The twist helps reinforce the tower. The Shanghai Tower needs 114 elevators, including the fastest elevator in the world.

Residents of the fourth tallest building in the world have no excuse for being late. The Makkah Royal Clock Tower, also known as the Abraj Al-Bait, in Mecca, Saudi Arabia, stands 1,972 feet (601 meters) tall. The building was completed in 2012, with a steel over concrete design. It holds apartments, hotels, and stores in its 120 stories. The four-faced clock on top is the highest and largest in the world. It can be seen from 16 miles (25 kilometers) away.

A full-time cleaning crew

Window washing on the Burj Khalifa is done four times a year. Each cleaning cycle takes three months, so crews are constantly cleaning it! The window washers get a great view, but working from that height must be scary.

Going up!

Another engineering challenge in megatall buildings is the elevators. Elevators run on steel cables, limiting the maximum height an elevator can reach to 1,640 feet (500 meters). Beyond that, steel cables may be unreliable. Engineers have proposed new kinds of elevators using carbon fiber cables or magnets to overcome this problem.

Merdeka 118

A tall dream

In 1957, American architect Frank Lloyd Wright designed a building that would have been over a mile high (1,600 meters). It was never built, but it would have been twice as tall as the Burj Khalifa.

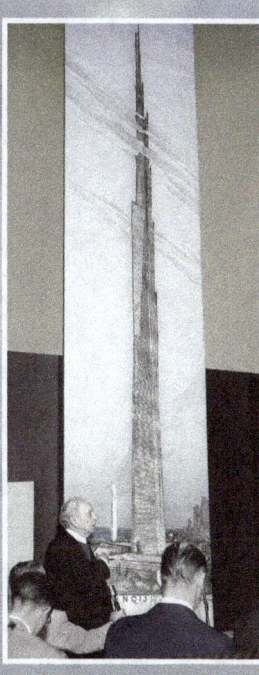

Paywalls:
Digital fences

Much of the internet is available for free. You don't have to pay to read a blog or watch YouTube. But sometimes you get a message that content is only available to subscribers. Those digital barriers, also known as paywalls, help content creators and publishers earn money for their work.

A paywall is a digital fence that restricts access to certain content on a website or app unless users pay a fee or subscribe. Paywalls are often used on websites operated by newspapers and media companies.

In the past, print newspapers and magazines made money by selling physical copies, subscriptions, and advertising space. In the digital age, paywalls were developed to encourage digital readers to financially support the people who create the online content they enjoy. They help news outlets pay the bills.

Paywalls operate in various ways. A website may allow users to view a limited number of articles free before being prompted to subscribe. This is called a metered paywall. With other paywalls, access is completely blocked, or the site may show the first few paragraphs of an article for free but restrict the rest to subscribers. Some websites have a selection of free articles but also paywalled sections with premium content for users who subscribe. Libraries often subscribe to digital publications, so card holders can get past the paywall if they access the publication through the library's portal.

The purpose of a paywall is to allow the people who produce the online content to be paid a fair wage for their creative work, so they can keep making more.

Original Sin

"Original Sin" is a joking term sometimes used to describe the decision by many news organizations to offer their content for free when the papers first went online. They believed that free online access would attract more print subscribers. But it didn't. Instead, it created the expectation that online content should always be free.

Blank Slate

Microsoft was one of the pioneers of the paywall model with their online magazine Slate in 1996. Annual subscriptions to Slate cost $19.95, about the same as a print magazine.

QR CODES:
The smartphone's short cut

Get your smartphone cameras ready! We are about to…read a menu? Check in at a doctor's appointment? Just point your camera at a QR code.

A QR code is a small square filled with a pattern of smaller squares. It may look random to you, but your smartphone reads it as a shortcut to a website or other information. A QR code is a type of barcode, a label that can be easily read by a computer. A traditional barcode is made up of lines or bars. You may have noticed them on packages. Stores use them to scan the prices of items at checkout. Many manufacturers use bar codes to sort parts.

Traditional barcodes can only store about 20 characters worth of information. Big factories often work with many parts—too many to be labeled with traditional bar codes. QR codes helped to solve this problem.

Tiny but mighty

QR codes can be smaller than barcodes. They can be printed on diamonds, fingernails, cookies, and small manufacturing parts. Feel free to take a bite of the cookie. QR codes can be accurately read even if they are damaged up to 30 percent.

Anatomy of a QR code

QR codes are made up of several elements. The larger squares help the phone to figure out the code's *orientation* (position). The tiny squares encode the data that makes each code unique.

QR stands for *quick response*.

Sky scan

Companies have created gigantic QR codes in fields bigger than football fields to promote products and services. But you must be on an airplane to scan them!

QR codes were invented in 1994 by the Japanese engineer Masahiro Hara. Their patterns can hold more than 7,000 digits of information and can be scanned in any direction.

QR codes were mainly used by manufacturers until the rise of smartphones in the early 2000's. Online companies realized that QR codes could also hold website addresses, or URL's. Point a phone camera at a code, and the phone's web browser goes to the website—no typing required.

RFID TAGS:
Invisible trackers

Have you ever seen cars speeding through a toll booth? The drivers are not cheating. The toll station recognized each vehicle and collected the payment automatically, with the help of RFID tags.

RFID (Radio Frequency Identification) tags are tiny chips that store small amounts of data. They can transmit information to an RFID reader using radio waves. RFID tags can be attached to products in a store, or embedded within credit cards, smartphones, key cards, and travel passes. They can even be implanted in plants or pets. They help organizations identify and track items as they move from place to place.

There are two types of RFID tags: passive and active. Passive tags have no battery and a maximum range of about 20 feet (6 meters). When a passive tag is scanned by an RFID reader, radio waves from the scanner activate the tag, giving it enough power to send information back. Passive tags are cheap and often used in stores.

Active tags have their own battery and a range of up to 1,500 feet (460 meters). Some, called beacons, automatically send out their information every few seconds. Others, called transponders, only send out their information when activated remotely. Active tags are used to collect tolls or track cargo or animals.

RFID tags can tell companies exactly how much stock they have in their warehouses. They can help farmers keep track of their livestock. They can help hospitals monitor the movements of patients, staff, and equipment. Chances are, you've met one today.

Radio key

In 1973, U.S. inventor Charles Walton designed a portable radio transmitter that could unlock a door. It worked by transmitting a signal to a reader next to the door. The technology was the basis for the RFID tag.

Farewell checkouts

In the future, you may be able to go to a supermarket, take the products you need, and leave without needing to pay for them at the checkout. Thanks to RFID technology, the store will deduct the amount you owe from your account automatically.

Streaming services:
Keep the media flowing

If you want to watch a movie, you could go out to a movie theater—or you could just stream one online. Streaming services deliver an endless supply of movies, music, and sports to screens around the world. But all those files don't live on your device.

Streaming technology allows users to listen to or view media while it is being transmitted rather than having to download a large media file. The streaming site breaks down content into small data packets, each containing a few seconds of video. These are sent one after another to the media player over the internet. Usually the packets disappear once they have played.

For this to work well, computers need to be able to send a lot of data very quickly. That means good bandwidth (how much data travels in a second). Improvements in data compression also help. Computer algorithms can use math to compress data into smaller file sizes, which are easier to transmit. But if an internet connection is slow, streaming video will sometimes pause while it waits for the next packets to arrive.

Before streaming services, users watched programs at set times on television. These were broadcast over radio waves or sent through cable. Then VCR's allowed users to record shows to watch when they wanted. The internet got fast enough to handle streaming video in the 2000's.

In 2005, the video-sharing website YouTube was launched. Now there are many streaming services to choose from, including Netflix, Hulu, Amazon Prime Video, Disney, and HBO. Even traditional television networks and movie studios have joined in. So much to watch, so little time!

Batter up

The first live-streaming event was a baseball game between the Seattle Mariners and the New York Yankees on September 5, 1995. Thousands of subscribers watched the game using Seattle-based startup RealNetworks's technology.

Streaming seesaw

A 2022 media report showed that younger people are more likely to subscribe, cancel, and return to a streaming service than older generations. Instead of paying all the time, these users subscribe to watch certain shows and then quit!

TIDAL ENERGY:
Power from the sea

Every day along coasts aound the world, the level of the ocean's surface rises and falls on a regular schedule once or twice a day. We call these the tides. Tidal motion is caused by the gravitational pull of the moon and sun. For centuries, people have wondered if it might be possible to harness the power of all that moving water. Now, we might be getting close.

How can tides generate electricity? With special tidal *turbines*, machines with blades that rotate as the water flows through them. The rotation powers a generator that produces electricity.

Different tidal energy projects use turbines in different ways. In a tidal stream generator, turbines sit under a floating platform attached to the seafloor or a bridge. When the tide flows in or out, moving water turns the turbine. Tidal stream generators work best in narrow channels, where the water flows faster.

A tidal barrage uses dams across tidal rivers, bays, and estuaries. Gates open as the tide rises, letting water in. At high tide, the gates close, trapping water behind the dam. This water is then released through turbines, producing energy at a controlled rate.

Tidal energy is clean and renewable, and tides are more dependable than wind and sunshine. But it is more expensive to build a tidal energy plant than to put up solar panels or wind turbines. Suitable locations are also limited. And some conservationists are concerned that underwater turbines or tidal dams could kill sea creatures, harm their habitat, and disrupt their navigation and communication.

Tidal lagoons

Tidal energy could also be captured using a tidal lagoon, a body of seawater separated from the sea by an artificial barrier that keeps out sea creatures but lets in rising and falling tides. Unlike barrages, tidal lagoons wouldn't disrupt marine life. Turbines in the barrier would generate electricity when the lagoon is filling and emptying.

Strangford Lough

The world's first tidal power station was built in 2008 at Strangford Lough in Northern Ireland. It has two turbines placed in a narrow strait and produces enough energy to power 1,500 households.

Video conferencing:
Making a remote connection

Going to a meeting no longer means sitting in a room with donuts. Now, it often means looking at people in tiles on a screen. Don't forget to unmute!

Video conferencing is a way to hold a meeting or catch up with friends remotely over a computer network. *Remote* means that the participants are not all in the same place. Instead, they share live audio and video. Video conferencing can help friends and families stay in touch and workers in different places *collaborate* (work together).

Group phone calls—called teleconferencing—have been around since the 1950's. But it wasn't until the 2000's that internet bandwidth became good enough to support real-time video chats.

In 2003, the chat service Skype allowed users to make audio calls between personal computers. Skype added video calling in 2005. Skype was developed to connect friends and family. But the service was quickly adopted by businesses to connect workers in different locations.

Video conferencing also allows users to show what's on their computer screen, called screen sharing. Meeting hosts can use screen sharing to show presentations or review documents with a team.

Hosting how-to

Preparing to host your first video meeting? First, create a meeting *agenda* (plan). List the topics that will be discussed at the meeting. Invite the participants via email and include the agenda. Set up for the meeting at a desk with good lighting. Minimize noisy distractions. Virtual backgrounds are available to blot out distracting surroundings. They can also make you look like you are in outer space!

In 2012, the video-calling software Zoom was released. In 2017, Microsoft introduced Teams, which includes video conferencing and chat.

When the COVID-19 *pandemic* (worldwide outbreak) shut down many offices beginning in 2020, video conferencing became a lifeline for businesses and schools. Authorities urged people to limit close personal contact to avoid spreading the illness. Video conferencing allowed workers to keep in touch and stay busy. Schools used video conferencing to teach classes online. Even after businesses reopened, video conferencing remains popular.

It is harder to share a box of donuts in a video meeting. But it's always nice to see a friendly face.

Fun features

Video conferencing keeps adding features. Some programs can provide real-time subtitles or translations. Many can filter out background noise and hide messy rooms. And there are tools for arranging groups, taking polls, and raising your hand to ask a question.

WIND FARMS:
Energy from the air

Wind is powerful. It can knock down trees and lift roofs off houses. For centuries, humans have used wind energy to propel ships, pump water, and grind grain. Today, we use it to make electricity, at wind farms.

A wind farm is an area that holds wind turbines—devices that can harvest the power of the wind. A wind turbine is a tall post supporting a set of blades that rotate when the wind flows past them. The spinning blades turn a magnet inside a copper coil, which generates electricity. This travels through wires to users.

Wind farms are usually located in windy areas on land or out at sea. Strong, steady winds that blow from one direction are best, since gusty winds can damage turbines. Mountain passes are ideal because winds tend to be stronger at high altitudes, especially when channeled through a narrow gap.

Offshore wind farms are built in the sea several miles or kilometers from the coast. Winds are stronger and more regular at sea because the wind moves more freely across flat water. Ocean wind farms near the shore (called inshore wind farms) sometimes get complaints from people who say they spoil the sea view. Offshore wind farms are farther away and less visible, but more expensive to build and maintain.

Wherever they spin, wind farms are a clean and renewable source of energy. They do not produce pollution or greenhouse gases. And crops can be grown on the land underneath—two farms in one.

Spacing the turbines

The spacing of turbines in a wind farm must be just right. Too close and the upwind turbines will block wind from the turbines to their rear. Too far apart and it raises the cost of building connecting roads and electric cables.

Biggest in the world

The largest wind farm in the world is the Gansu Wind Farm in Gansu, China, which had a capacity of 7.9 gigawatts in 2023, enough to power almost six million homes. The world's biggest offshore wind farm is Hornsea Wind Farm off the coast of the UK, which has 165 wind turbines and produces enough power for around 1.4 million homes.

Index

Abraj Al-Bait (skyscraper), 62
air purification, 20-21
Anderson, Robert (inventor), 35
Apollo 15 (moon mission), 35
Apple (company), 39, 46, 59
Apple Pay (payment service), 39
artificial intelligence (AI), 14-15, 22

bioink, 7
Bitcoin, 13, 28-29
blockchain, 12-13, 28
Boeri, Stefano (architect), 43
bullet trains, 57
Burj Khalifa (skyscraper), 60, 62-63

Cairos (software), 45
CAPTCHA's, 14-15
carbon, 16-17, 30, 36, 41-42, 50-51, 53, 63
carbon capture, 16-17
carbon dioxide (CO_2), 16-17, 36, 42, 53
carbon fiber, 30, 63
Cash App (payment service), 38-39
cellular service, 8-9
chip cards, 18-19

coal, 21, 36
computer-aided design, 4
computer image recognition, 22-25
convolutional neural networks (CNN's), 22, 24
COVID-19 pandemic, 27, 75
coworking spaces, 26-27
cryptocurrency, 13, 28-29, 39
Curiosity (rover), 23

Davenport, Thomas (inventor), 35
desertification, 52-53
direct air capture (DAC), 16-17
drones, 30-33

electric vehicles (EV's), 34-37, 42
electronic payments, 38-39
encryption, 9, 13, 28

facial recognition, 25
fifth-generation (5G) wireless, 8-9
forest cities, 42-43
fourth-generation (4G) wireless, 9
Fuller, Buckminster (inventor), 49

Gansu Wind Farm, 77
Geim, Andre (scientist), 51
goal-line technology (GLT), 44-45
Goldberg, David (scientist), 48
Gorilla Glass, 46-47
Gott, J. Richard (scientist), 48
Gott-Goldberg-Vanderbei projection, 48-49
graphene, 50-51
graphite, 51
Great Green Wall, 52-53
Great Pyramid of Giza, 61

Haber, Stuart (researcher), 13
Hara, Masahiro (engineer), 67
Hawk Eye (software), 44-45
HEPA filters, 20
high-speed rail (HSR), 54-57
Home Life Insurance building, 60
Hornsea Wind Farm, 77

Jobs, Steve (entrepreneur), 46

Kirsch, Russell A. (scientist), 25

laptops, 58-59
latency, 9
lithium batteries, 34, 36, 50
Liuzhou forest city, 42
Lunar Roving Vehicle, 35

MacBook Air, 59
maglev trains, 54-55
magnetic-stripe cards, 18-19
Makkah Royal Clock Tower (skyscraper), 62
Massachusetts Institute of Technology (MIT), 32
megatall skyscrapers, 60-63
Mercator projection, 48
Merdeka 118 (skyscraper), 62-63
microplastics, 10-11
Microsoft (company), 65, 75
Mr. Trash Wheel (cleanup device), 10-11

Nakamoto, Satoshi (creator of Bitcoin), 29
Novoselov, Konstantin (scientist), 51

Ocean Health Lab, 11
optical character recognition (OCR), 24
Osborne 1 (computer), 59

PayPal (payment service), 38-39
paywalls, 64-65
pollution, 10-11, 20-21, 36, 42, 76
Proteus (solar power system), 41

QR codes, 66-67

radio waves, 8-9, 68-70
recurrent neural networks (RNN's), 24
RFID tags, 68-69

Sahara (desert), 52
Sahel (region in Africa), 52
Seabin (cleanup device), 10
Shanghai Tower (skyscraper), 61-62
skyscrapers, 17, 60-63
smog, 20-21
solar panels, 40-42
solar power, 10, 20, 40-42
Stornetta, W. Scott (researcher), 13
streaming services, 70-71
superconductivity, 54-55

Tesla, Nikola (inventor), 33
three-dimensional (3D) printing, 4-7, 27

tidal barrages, 72-73
tidal energy, 72-73
tidal lagoons, 73
trash, in oceans, 10-11
triangulation, 44
turbines, 72-73, 76-77,
Turing, Alan (computer pioneer), 15

unmanned aerial vehicles (UAV's), 30-33

Vanderbei, Robert (scientist), 48-49
Venmo (payment service), 38-39
video conferencing, 74-75

Walton, Charles (inventor), 69
water cleanup, 10-11
wind farms, 76-77
wind turbines, 76-77
World Health Organization (WHO), 20
Wright, Frank Lloyd (architect), 63

Zelle (payment service), 39

Acknowledgments

Cover © guteksk7/Shutterstock; © metamorworks/Shutterstock; © nutroza/Shutterstock; © Dabarti CGI/Shutterstock; © Iurii Motov, Shutterstock; © koonsiri boonnak/Shutterstock; © TTstudio/Shutterstock; © Volodymyr Burdiak, Shutterstock; © ssguy/Shutterstock; © whiteMocca/Shutterstock

4-5 © Natalia Arefieva, Shutterstock; © belekekin/Shutterstock

6-7 © guteksk7/Shutterstock; © Sergey Kolesnikov, Shutterstock; © luchschenF/Shutterstock

8-9 © ustas7777777/Shutterstock; © Steve Broer, Shutterstock; © Marko Aliaksandr, Shutterstock; © metamorworks/Shutterstock

10-11 © Tippa Patt, Shutterstock; © Dmytro Surkov, Shutterstock; © smereka/Shutterstock; © rangizzz/Shutterstock

12-13 © LuckyStep/Shutterstock; © whiteMocca/Shutterstock; © Coyz0/Shutterstock; © elenabsl/Shutterstock; © Leo Wolfert, Shutterstock

14-15 © lilgrapher/Shutterstock; © Lenscap Photography/Shutterstock; © metrue/Shutterstock; © Sunward Art/Shutterstock

16-17 © Clare Louise Jackson, Shutterstock; © nnattalli/Shutterstock; © Keshi Studio/Shutterstock; © Grand Warszawski/Shutterstock

18-19 © Nils Z/Shutterstock; © Ground Picture/Shutterstock

20-21 © Abaca Press/Alamy Images; © kheartmanee thongyot/Shutterstock; © Imaginechina Limited/Alamy Images; © Phil Watson Photography/Shutterstock

22-23 © RioAbajoRio/Shutterstock; © Dabarti CGI/Shutterstock; © Dima Zel, Shutterstock

24-25 © AlinStock/Shutterstock; © TimeStopper69/Shutterstock; © metamorworks/Shutterstock

26-27 © Monkey Business Images/Shutterstock; © Modest Things/Shutterstock; © leungchopan/Shutterstock

28-29 © Gorodenkoff/Shutterstock; © Carlos Castilla/Shutterstock; © Mykhaylo Kozelko, Shutterstock; © Kitti Suwanekkasit/Shutterstock

30-31 © fokke baarssen/Shutterstock; © Goinyk Production/Shutterstock; © Juttni-virk/Shutterstock

32-33 © Scharfsinn/Shutterstock; Public Domain; MIT; © SizeSquares/Shutterstock; © Tibbut Archive/Alamy Images

34-35 © DG FotoStock/Shutterstock; © Darunrat Wongsuvan, Shutterstock; © Castleski/Shutterstock

36-37 © CoreDESIGN/Shutterstock; © nutroza/Shutterstock; © IM Imagery/Shutterstock; © Ilija Erceg, Shutterstock

38-39 © TStudious/Shutterstock; © Ken Wolter, Shutterstock; © Golden Dayz/Shutterstock; © marog - pixcells/Shutterstock; © Iurii Motov, Shutterstock

40-41 © korinnna/Shutterstock; © Avigator Fortuner/Shutterstock; © SolarisFloat

42-43 © Stefano Boeri Architetti; © Todamo/Shutterstock; © leolintang/Shutterstock

44-45 © janews/Shutterstock; © kitti Suwanekkasit, Shutterstock; © Fotosr52/Shutterstock; © sezer66/Shutterstock

46-47 © Alexandra Morosanu/Shutterstock; © asharkyu/Shutterstock; © RHJPhtotos/Shutterstock; © Mitzxxz/Shutterstock

48-49 Robert J. Vanderbei, Princeton; © Triff/Shutterstock; NASA

50-51 © ktsdesign/Shutterstock; © Marco de Benedictis, Shutterstock; © Production Perig/Shutterstock; © maodoltee/Shutterstock; © Lightboxx/Shutterstock; © BONNINSTUDIO/Shutterstock; © Irmun/Shutterstock

52-53 © aphotostory/Shutterstock; © natthawut.2529/Shutterstock; © Georg Gerster, Science Source

54-55 © l i g h t p o e t/Shutterstock; © cyo bo/Shutterstock; © Hung Chung Chih, Shutterstock; © AlexLMX/Shutterstock

56-57 © ArtisticPhoto/Shutterstock; © EvergreenPlanet/Shutterstock; © ssguy/Shutterstock

58-59 © CHUYKO SERGEY/Shutterstock; © Gado Images/Alamy Images; © TippaPatt/Shutterstock; © Jim Goldstein, Alamy Images; © Andrey Popov, Shutterstock; © CHALERMCHAI99/Shutterstock

60-61 © Gensler; © TTstudio/Shutterstock; © Photo Hedge/Shutterstock; © Alex Anton, Shutterstock

62-63 Library of Congress; © Uskarp/Shutterstock; © Osama Ahmed Mansour, Shutterstock; © Pixeljunkie19/Shutterstock; Milkomde (licensed under CC BY-SA 4.0); © From Original Negative/Alamy Images

64-65 © BestForBest/Shutterstock; © maxicam/Shutterstock; © Linaimages/Shutterstock; © phoelixDE/Shutterstock

66-67 © dpa picture alliance archive/Alamy Images; © Xinhua/Alamy Images; © Kirill Neiezhmakov, Shutterstock; © shisu_ka/Shutterstock; © 4045/Shutterstock

68-69 © Albert Lozano, Shutterstock; © Ireshetnikov54/Shutterstock; © Koonsiri Boonnak, Shutterstock; © metamorworks/Shutterstock; © Chutima Chaochaiya, Shutterstock

70-71 © ymgerman/Shutterstock; © Budrul Chukrut, Shutterstock; © Proxima Studio/Shutterstock; © Ronnie Chua, Shutterstock

72-73 © Breedfoto/Shutterstock; © Girl Grace, Shutterstock; © Alex Mit, Shutterstock; © Francois Boizot, Shutterstock

74-75 © Vadym Pastukh, Shutterstock; © fizkes/Shutterstock

76-77 © Volodymyr Burdiak, Shutterstock; © Matyas Rehak, Shutterstock; © Nuttawut Uttamaharad, Shutterstock; © Ryan Conine, Shutterstock

www.ingramcontent.com/pod-product-compliance
Lightning Source LLC
Chambersburg PA
CBHW080922180426
43192CB00040B/2665